Bubbles and Friends

Sandra L. Ross

Copyright © 2024 by Sandra Ross

All rights reserved. No part of this publication may be reproduced, distributed or transmitted in any form or by any means, including photocopying, recording, or other electronic or mechanical methods, without the prior written permission of the publisher, except in the case of brief quotations embodied in critical reviews and certain other noncommercial uses permitted by copyright law. For permission requests, write to the publisher, addressed "Attention: Permissions Coordinator," at the address below.

Sandra Ross/Rejoice Essential Publishing
PO BOX 512
Effingham, SC 29541
www.republishing.org

Bubbles and Friends/Sandra Ross
ISBN-13: 979-8-3304-3023-9

Dedication

Some friends are fun to be with, but a loyal friend can be better than a brother. — (Proverbs 18:24 ERV)

Hello, I'm Bubbles the Duck and I live on a farm with my special friends. I start each day visiting my friends and you're welcome to come along. My friends would love to meet you.

"Cockle Doodle Doo! Good Morning! Rise and Shine!," says Rowdy Rooster as he stands on top of the hen house.

The farm comes alive, and you hear all the animals wake up and start their day.

"Oink, Oink," as the pigs roll in the mud and "Quack, Quack," as the ducks run to the pond.

"Good morning, Rowdy Rooster," says Bubbles. Rowdy Rooster is a little grumpy and mumbles, "I'm tired! Dick the Sly Fox kept trying to steal eggs from the chicken coop all night."

Bubbles try to cheer him up, but nothing works. Bubbles reaches into his backpack and gives Rowdy Rooster a bottle labeled, "Happiness." He blows big funny shaped bubbles and does a dance. Rowdy Rooster starts laughing so much that he forgets about being grumpy.

"Bubbles, Bubbles, Bye!" Bubbles waves at Kathy as she gets on the school bus. Kathy is the farmer's daughter and she's in the first grade. Every morning, Bubbles waits with her for the bus to arrive. All the kids love Bubbles because he blows animal shaped bubbles that make them laugh and they forget they had to wake up so early.

Next Bubbles visits Callie the Cow and he waves and says, "Good Morning on this lovely day." "Moo! Moo! The sun is bright today and whew, there's flies everywhere and my poor tail is tired from fanning them away," says Callie the Cow. Bubbles reaches into his backpack and gives her a yellow bracelet that keeps the bugs away.

"Moo! Moo!" Callie is so happy that she gives Bubbles a jar of her special milk. Callie is a unique cow because her milk is pink and tastes like strawberries. Bubbles gulps the milk all down and says, "Yummy!," while rubbing his belly.

"Baa, Baa!" Oh, look, that's Eva the Diva Sheep and she's won every beauty contest for the last four years. "Good morning, Eva. You're pretty as always." "Thank You Bubbles and hello to our new friend and what's your name?"

(_____)

(add your name)

Welcome to a day full of fun adventures on our happy farm. Bubbles says bye to Eva and gives her a bouquet of colorful flowers from his backpack. Bubbles thank you for visiting me and making me feel beautiful.

"Who's that walking on tippy toes?" says, _____.
(Add Your Name)

That's Dick the Slick Fox and he's heading toward the chicken coop again. Bubbles shouts, "Good Morning Dick!" and the Sly Fox stops in his tracks and turns around.

"Well Good Morning Bubbles. I didn't think anyone could see me." Bubbles tells Dick the Sly Fox that Rowdy Rooster is on the look out for him. The Fox looks scared and starts trembling.

Bubbles reaches into his backpack and gives him a piece of bread with honey. Dick the Sly Fox starts giggling because he hasn't had breakfast yet and is hungry. "Thank You Bubbles, for being a good friend and next time, I'll treat you to breakfast. Well, I better get going before it rains, or Rowdy Rooster sees me."

"Look Out! Look Out!" As a hockey disc flies over Bubbles' head. "Wow! That was too close." "I apologize," says Bobby the Canadian Goose. "Hi Bobby, who's winning?" "We are of course, despite being hot today. My team needs all the practice we can get to win the championship again."

Bubbles tells Bobby, "We're heading back before it rains. Are you coming?" "No, there's only a few months before we'll be flying back to Canada."

Bubbles reaches into his backpack and gives Bobby the Goose a cold bottle of water to help cool him down and waves. "Bye. See you later."

Bubbles tells Bobby, "We're heading back before it rains. Are you coming?" "No, there's only a few months before we'll be flying back to Canada."

Bubbles reaches into his backpack and gives Bobby the Goose a cold bottle of water to help cool him down and waves. "Bye. See you later."

As Bubbles and his new friend head towards the farm, they see Neal the Smart horse and Bubbles waves and says, "Hello." Neal says, "Neigh, Neigh! I have a full class today and they're full of energy." Neal teaches all the farm animals and we're the smartest farm in the area.

Bubbles reaches into his backpack and gives him a bright red apple and blows bubbles before leaving. Thank you Bubbles for being a thoughtful friend.

Did you enjoy visiting my friends today? To be a friend, you must be friendly and treat everyone the way you want to be treated. A little kindness goes a long way.

The End

www.ingramcontent.com/pod-product-compliance
Lightning Source LLC
LaVergne TN
LVHW081454060526
838201LV00050BA/1798